Women Napping
with Animals

Poems by
Anna Broome

~

Illustrations by
Ted Meyer

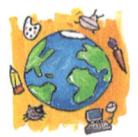

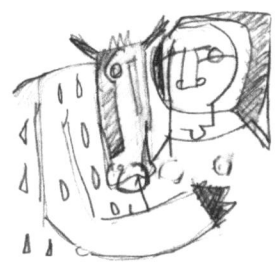

Toes tucked in
eyes closed shut
a day is ending

dreams are beginning

lights turned off
bed untucked
body disappearing

mind is streaming

napping with animals
brings good luck
the morning is coming

It's time to get up

Bovine and Divine

Bull and Lady Dai
both cave art dwellers
share 40 winks
17,000 years later

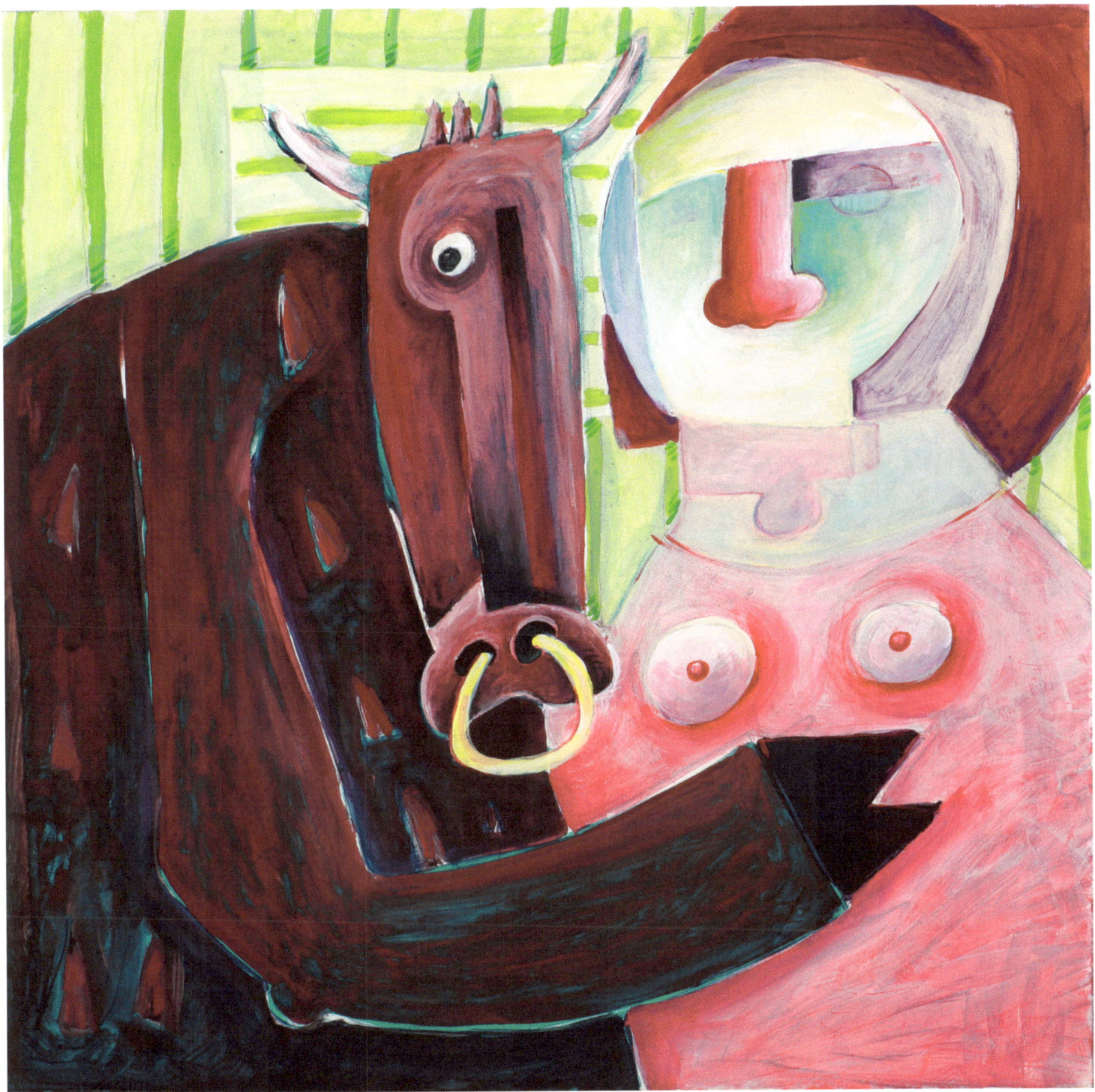

Goat or Nymph

Matisse's muse
and Thor's chariot lead
called in infirm
as subterfuge

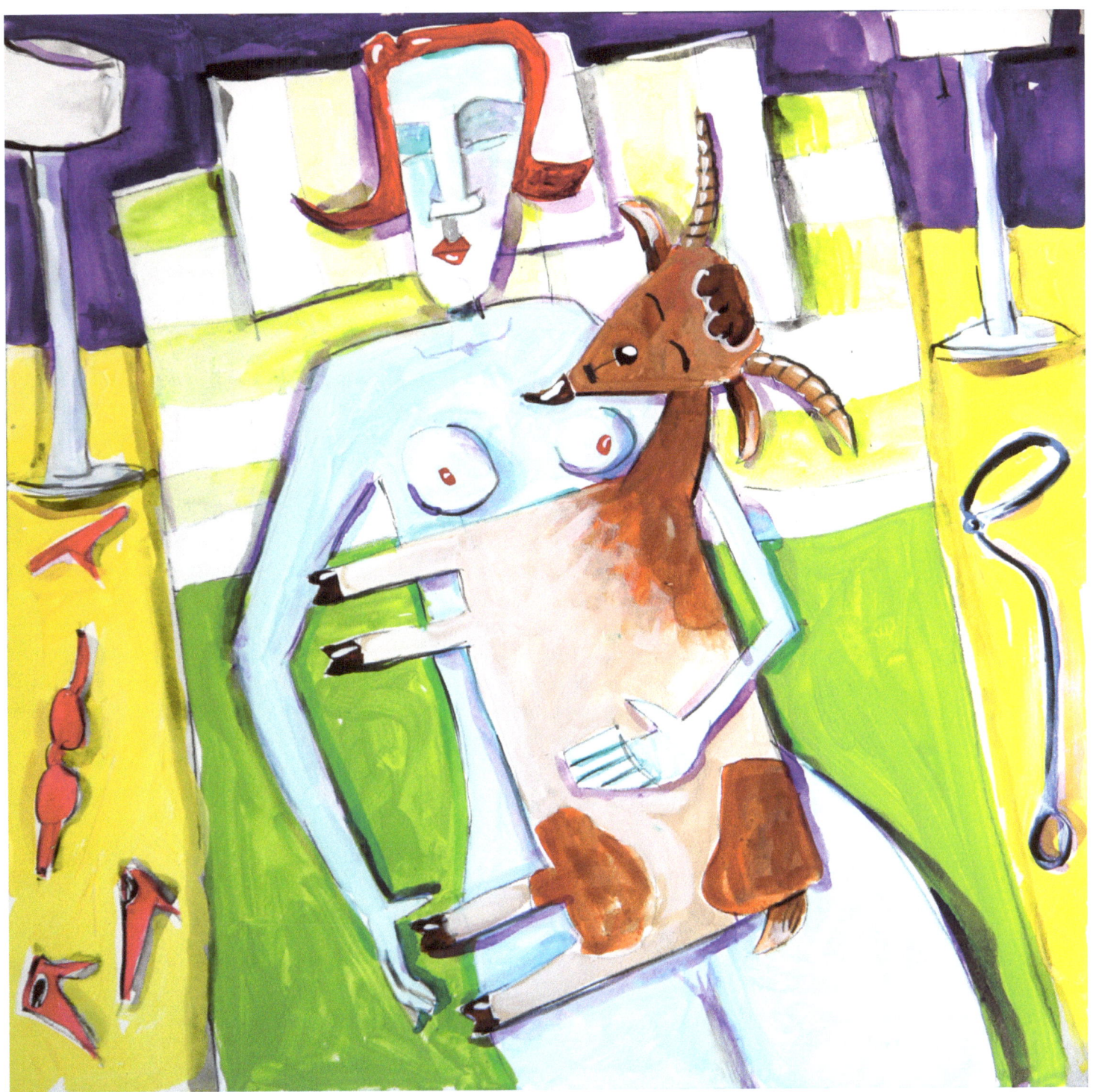

Chickadee

Clucked out inside
a Kentucky Duchess box
a tender chicken
hidden from the fox

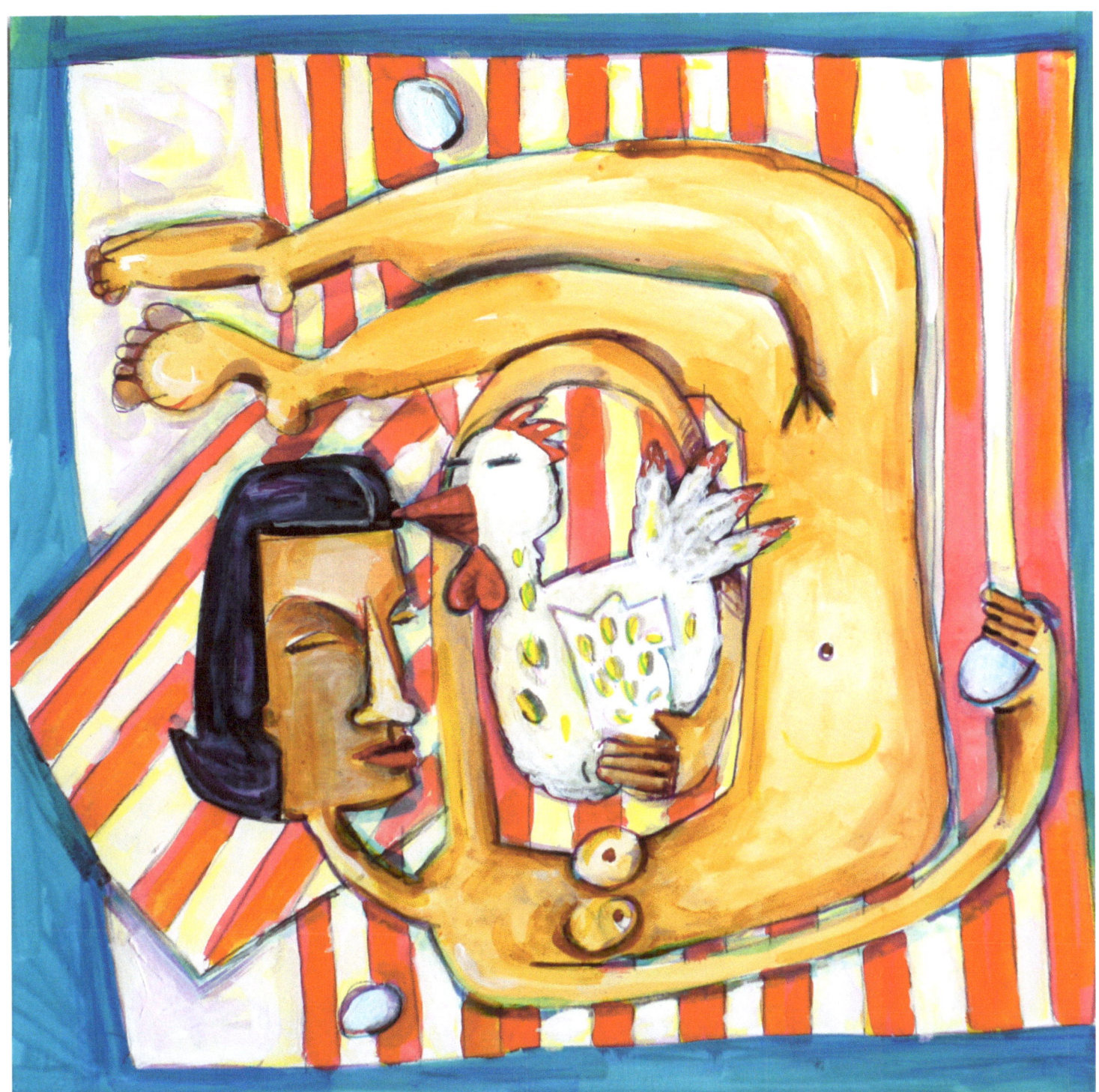

Nubian Tomb

Brought to a sleep temple,
folded in half
an Egyptian Ruler and a giraffe

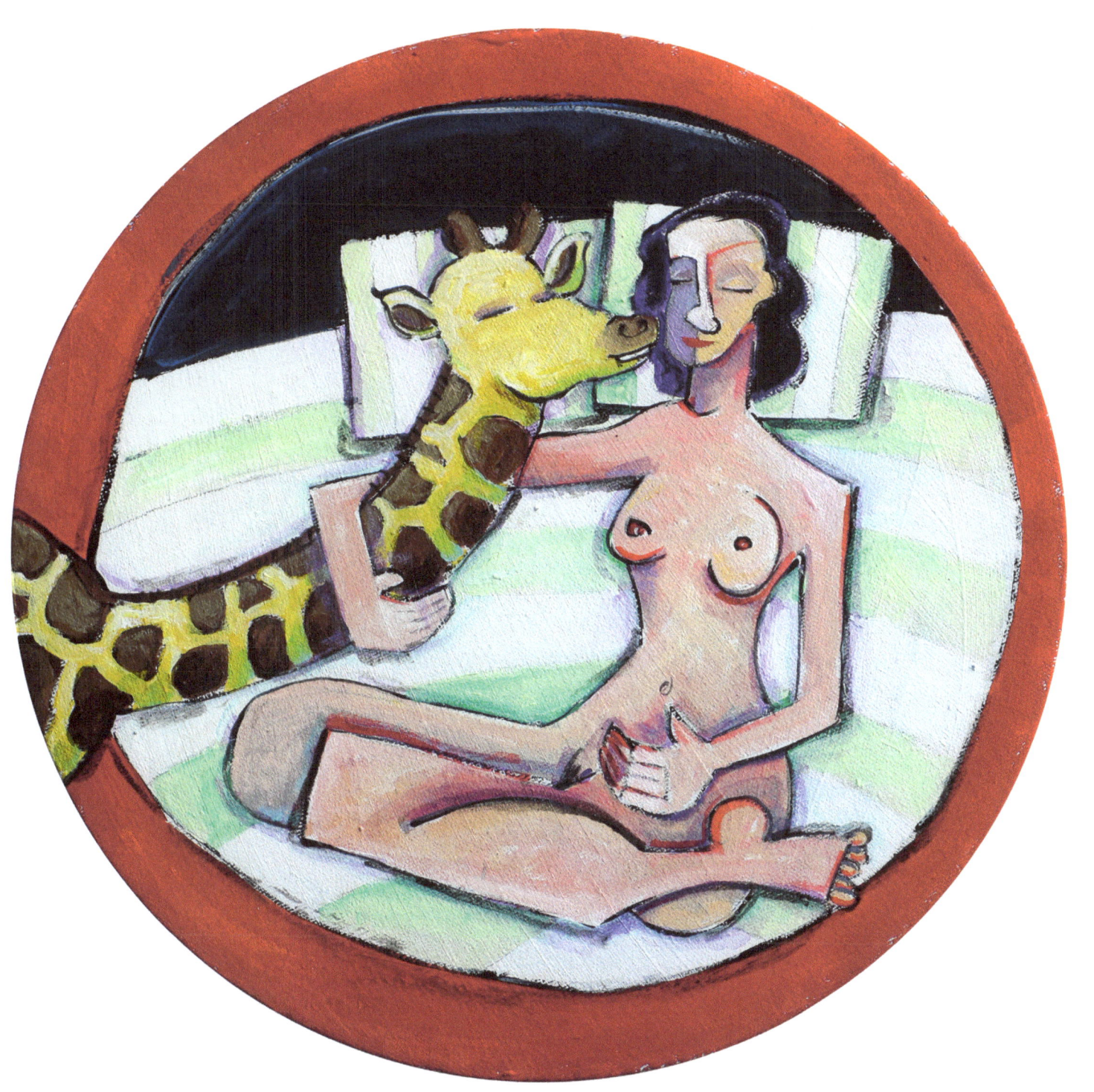

Cherry Lipstick and Octopus

My one-eyed gypsy holds me round,
and round pulls me deep below the ocean's surface,
separates me from sound

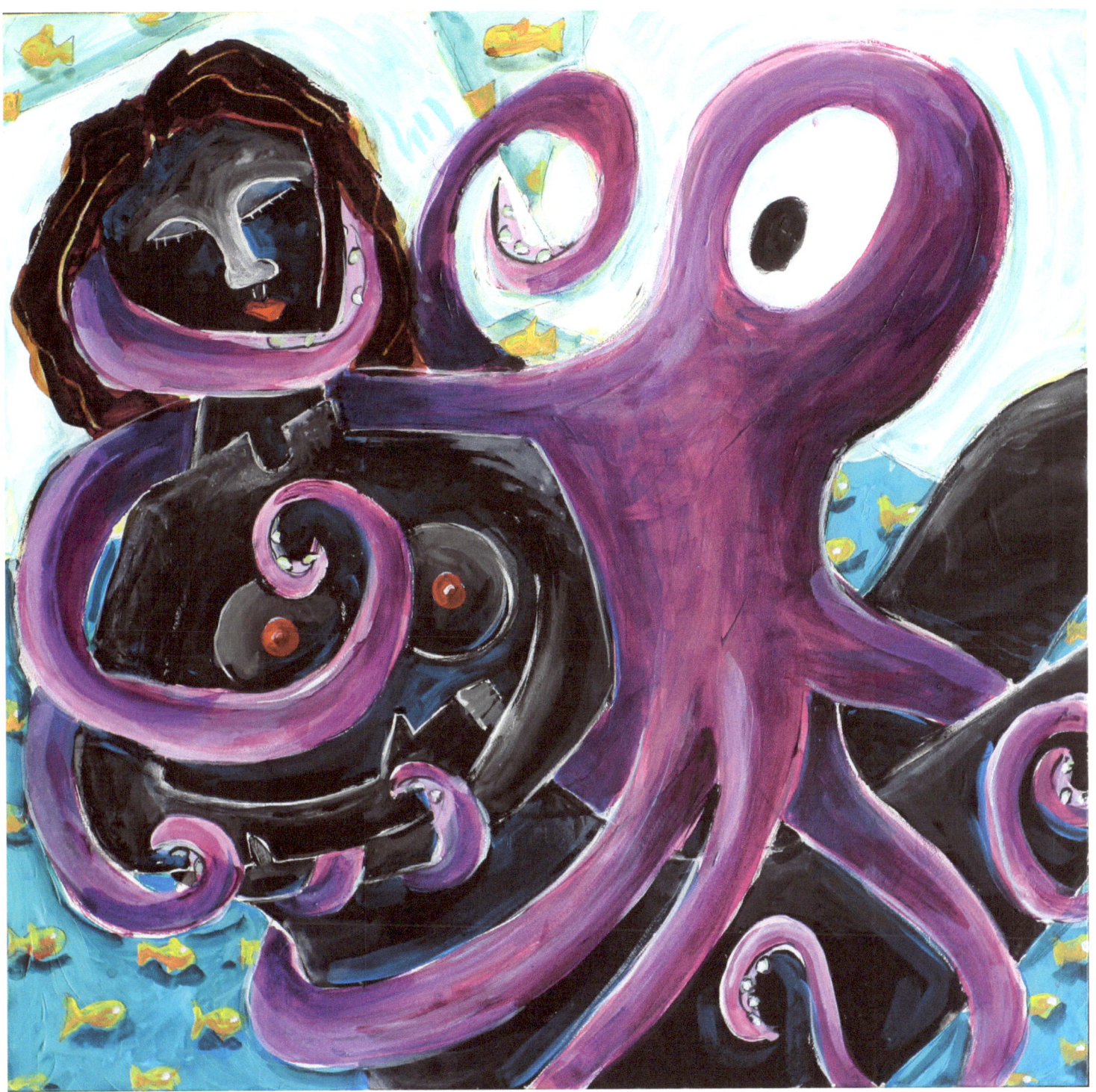

Fowl Pride

Hera, Queen of the Heavens beside
her Prince of Peacock pride
are ancient sleeping friends
protected by many watchful eyes

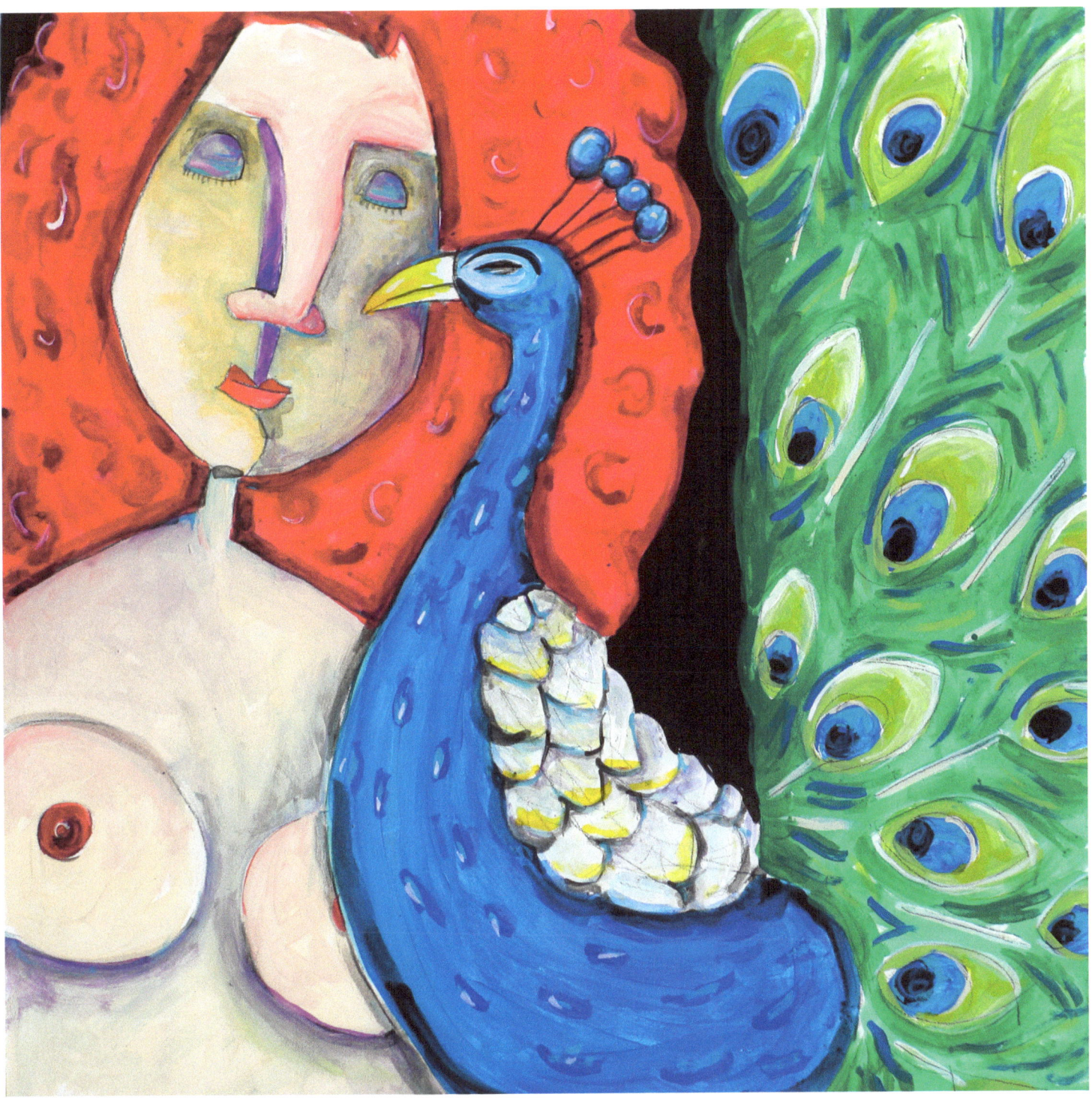

Fraternal Purr

Kittens as mittens
as a soft sleep attire
is all this lover of felines
requires to retire

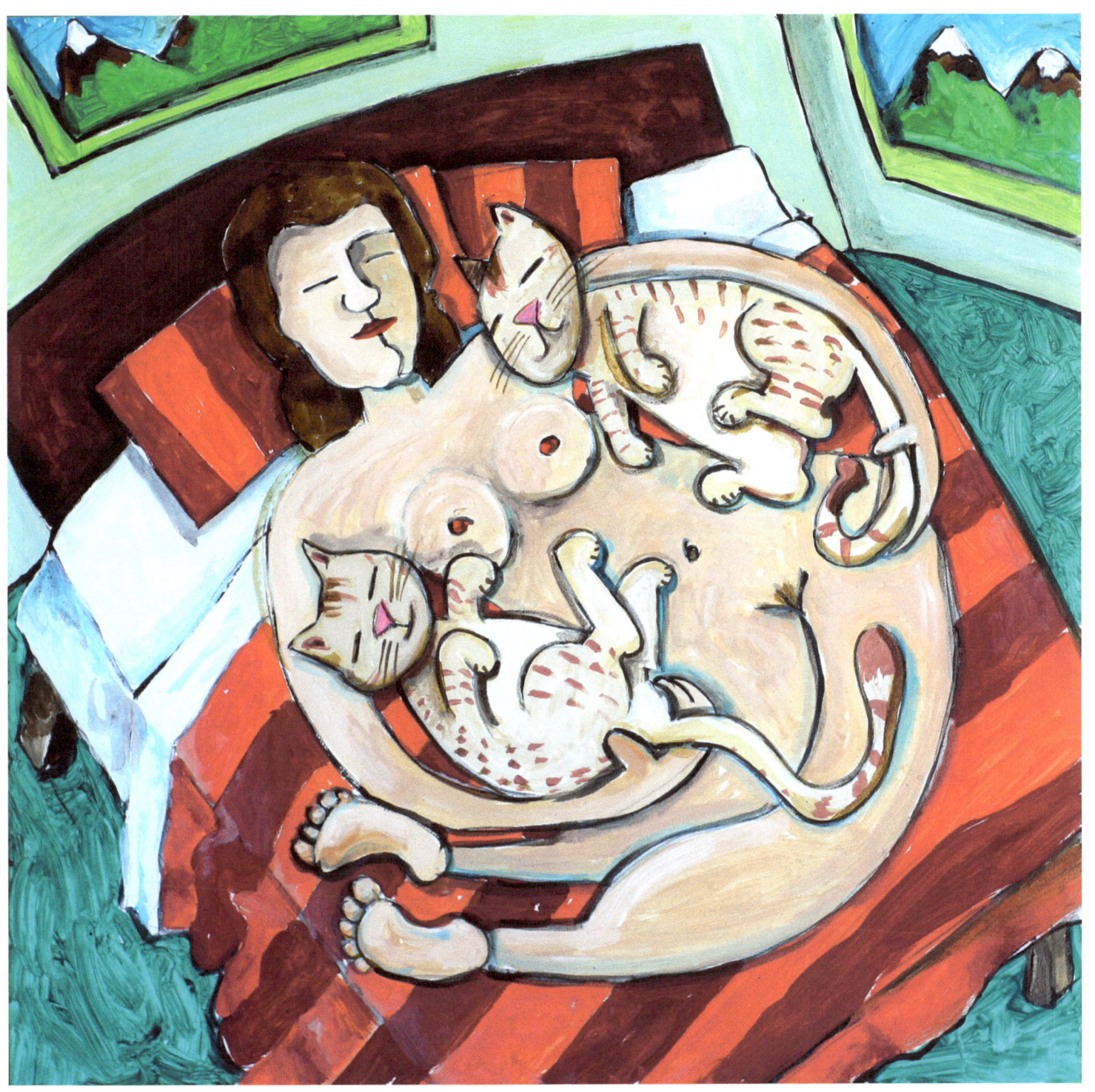

Matriarchs

Remembering even in dreams
how long a night seems
under a crater moon
when no one wakes before noon

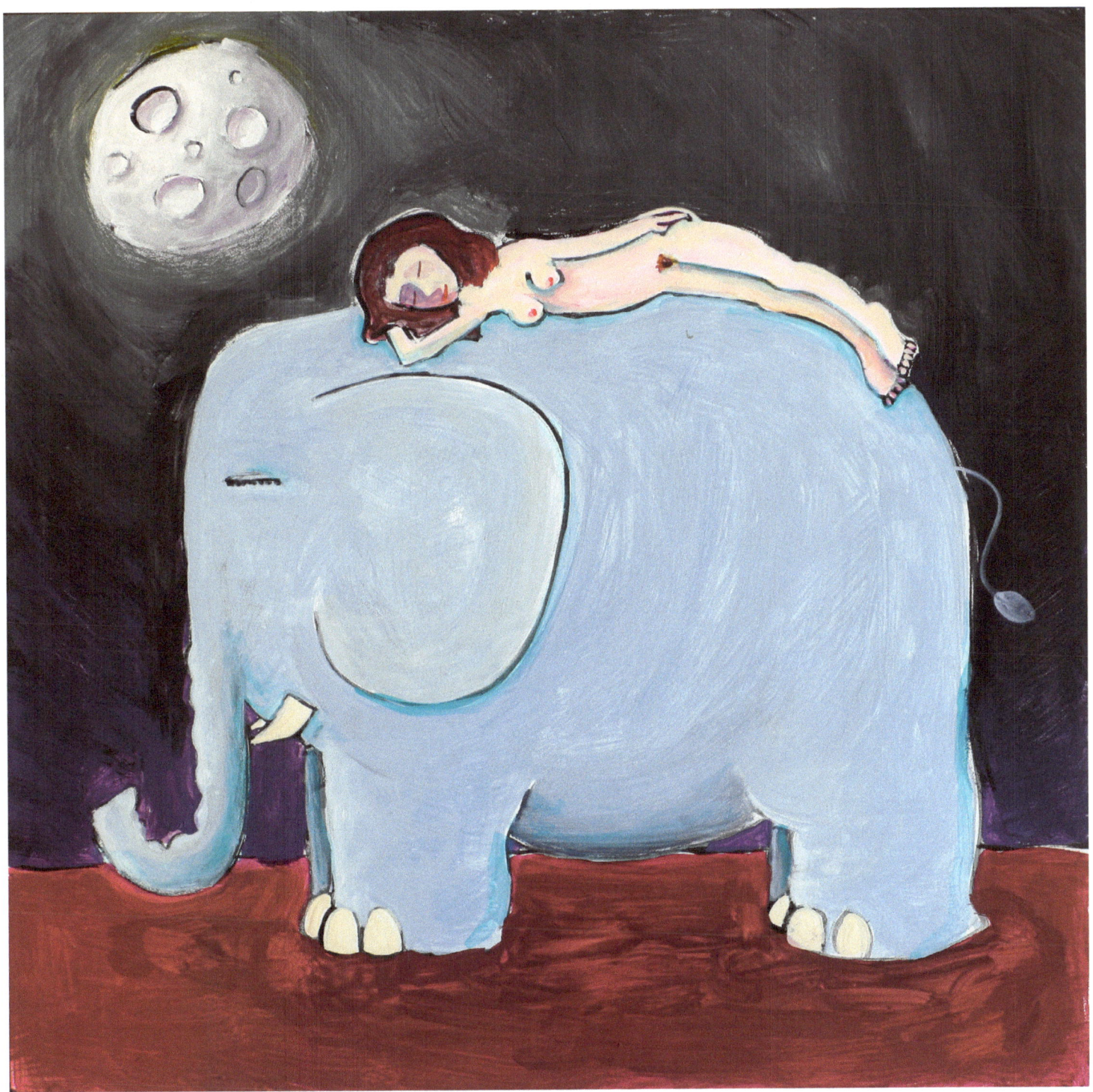

Hops and Chops

Sleeping made them thirsty,
and drinking made them sleepy...
a vicious cycle for girl and puppy

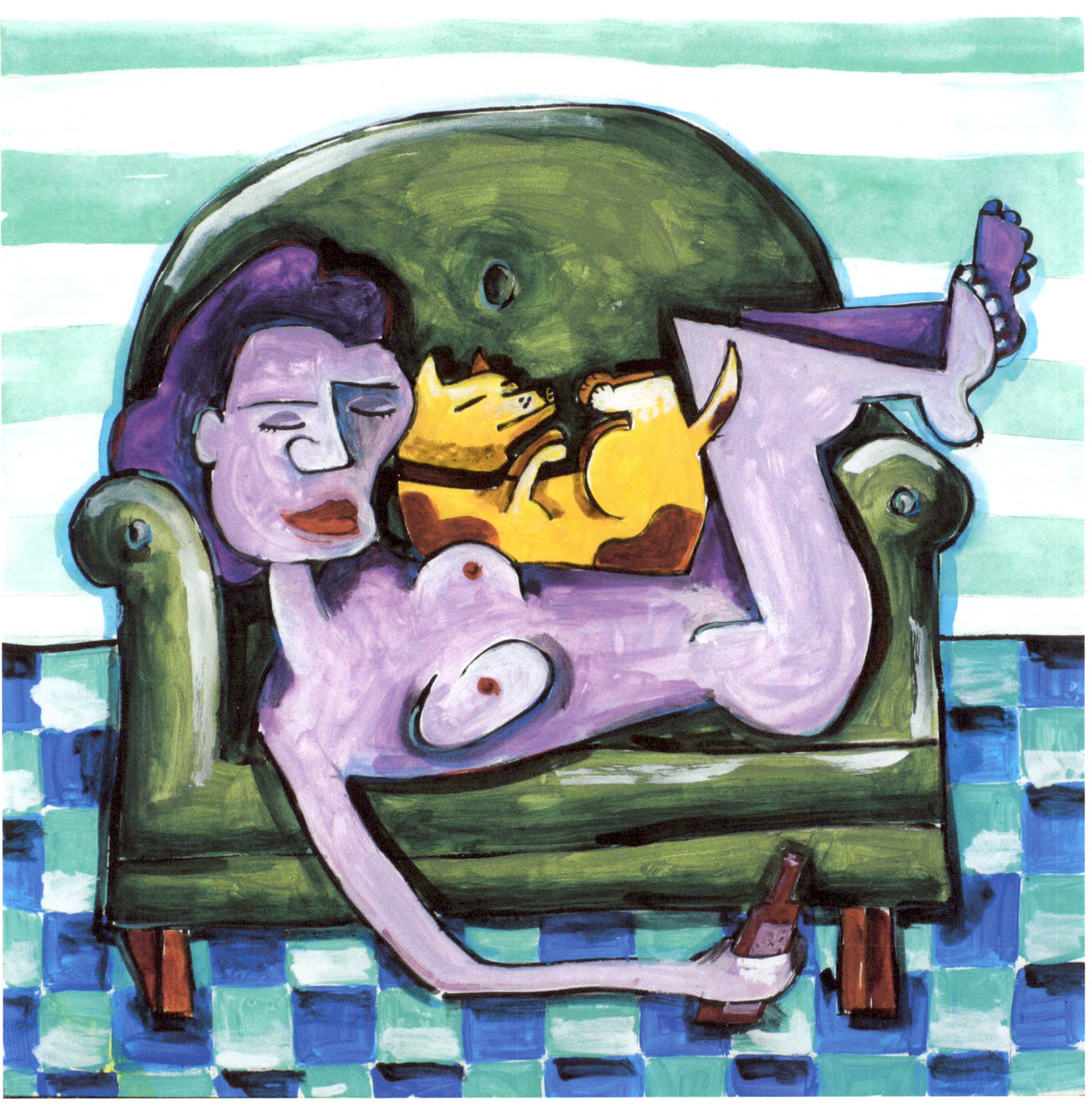

Bear and Babes

Deep in winter
two girls and their bear slumber
won't hear the phone ring
until they wake up later in Spring

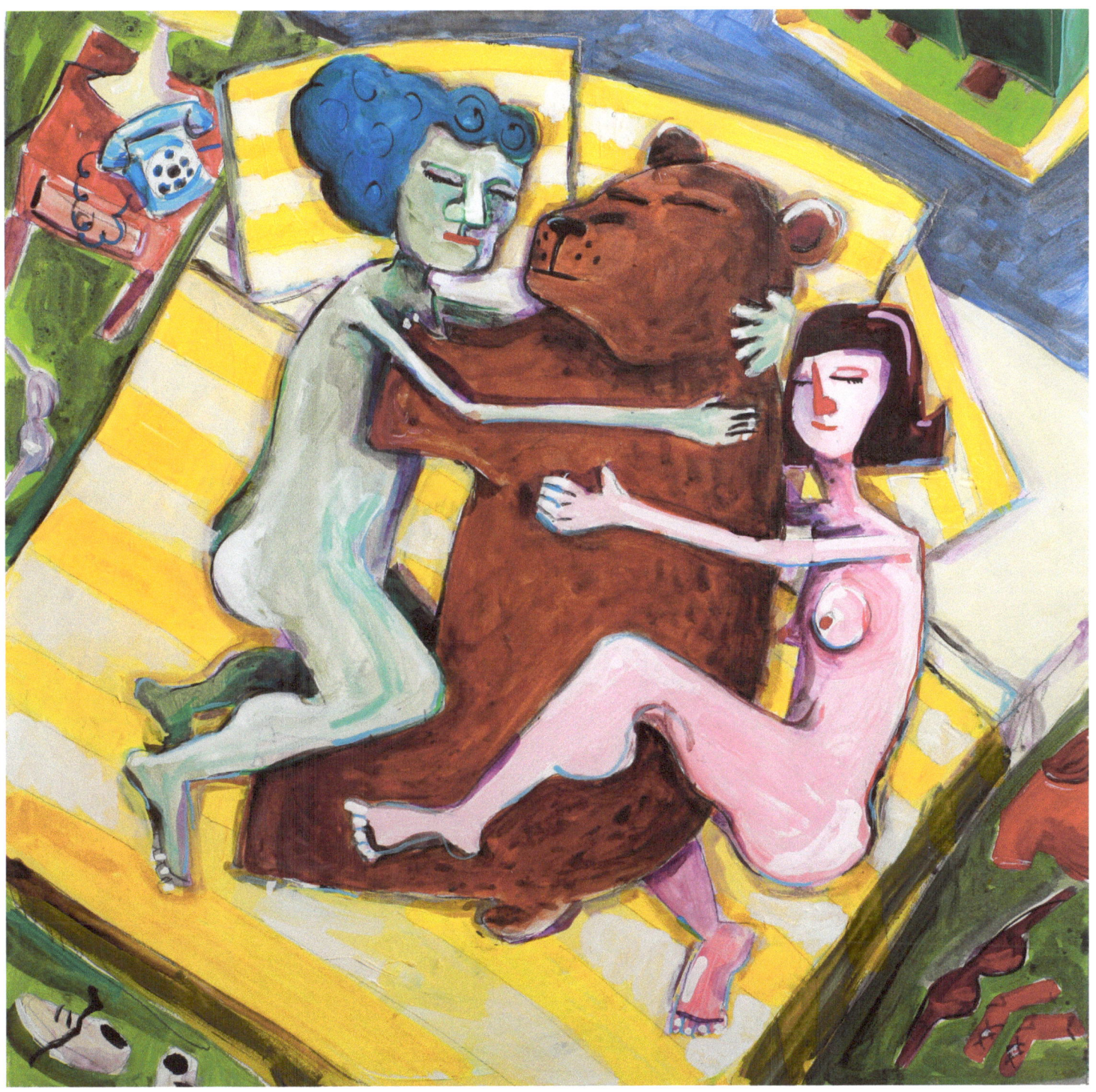

Moo Shoo

Idol cow and idle woman
milk a masked third
and form a coven

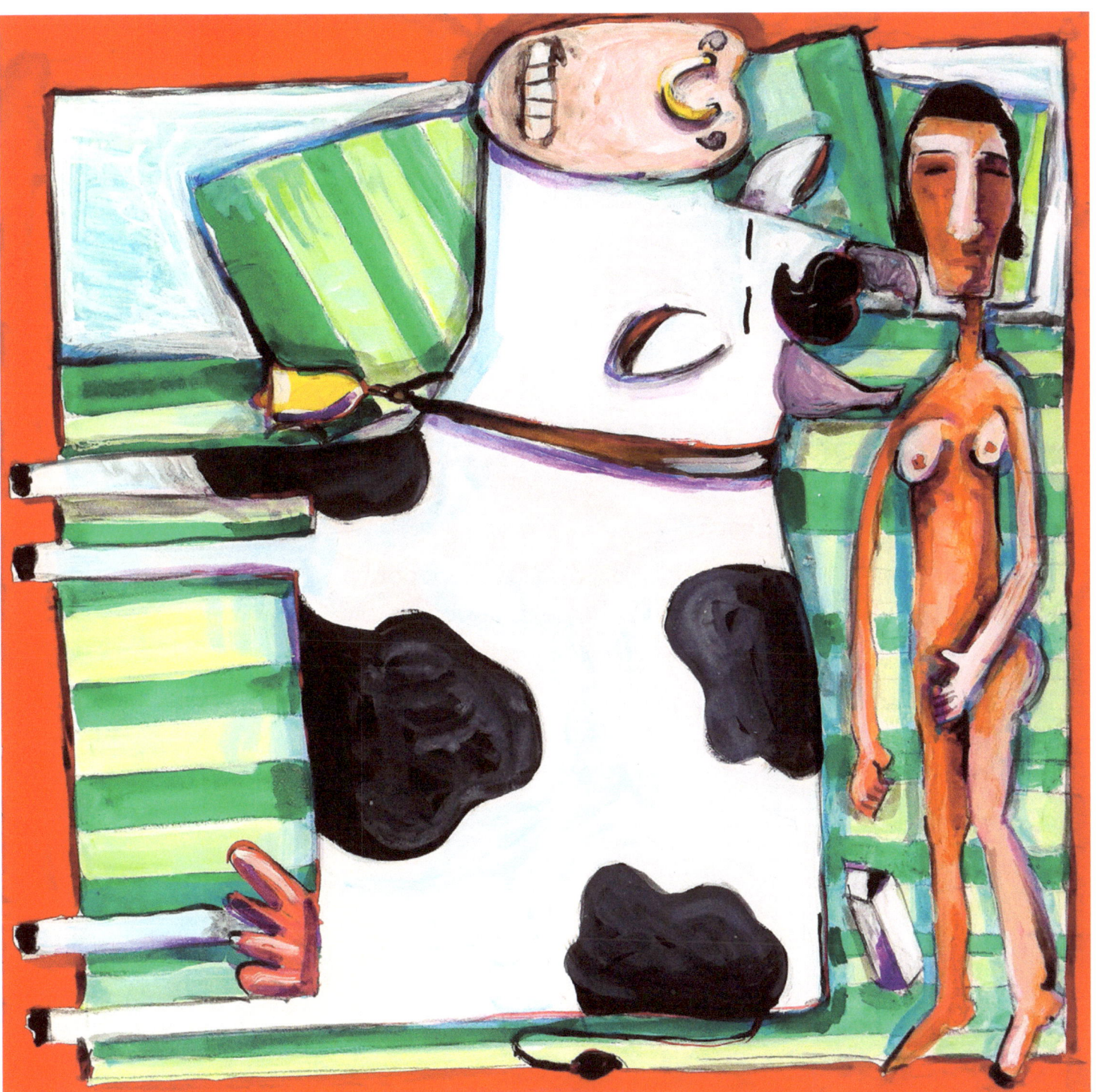

Hippo Hero

The eponymous hero
for the Maiden Woo her hippopotamus
will charge tomorrow
when his nap is through

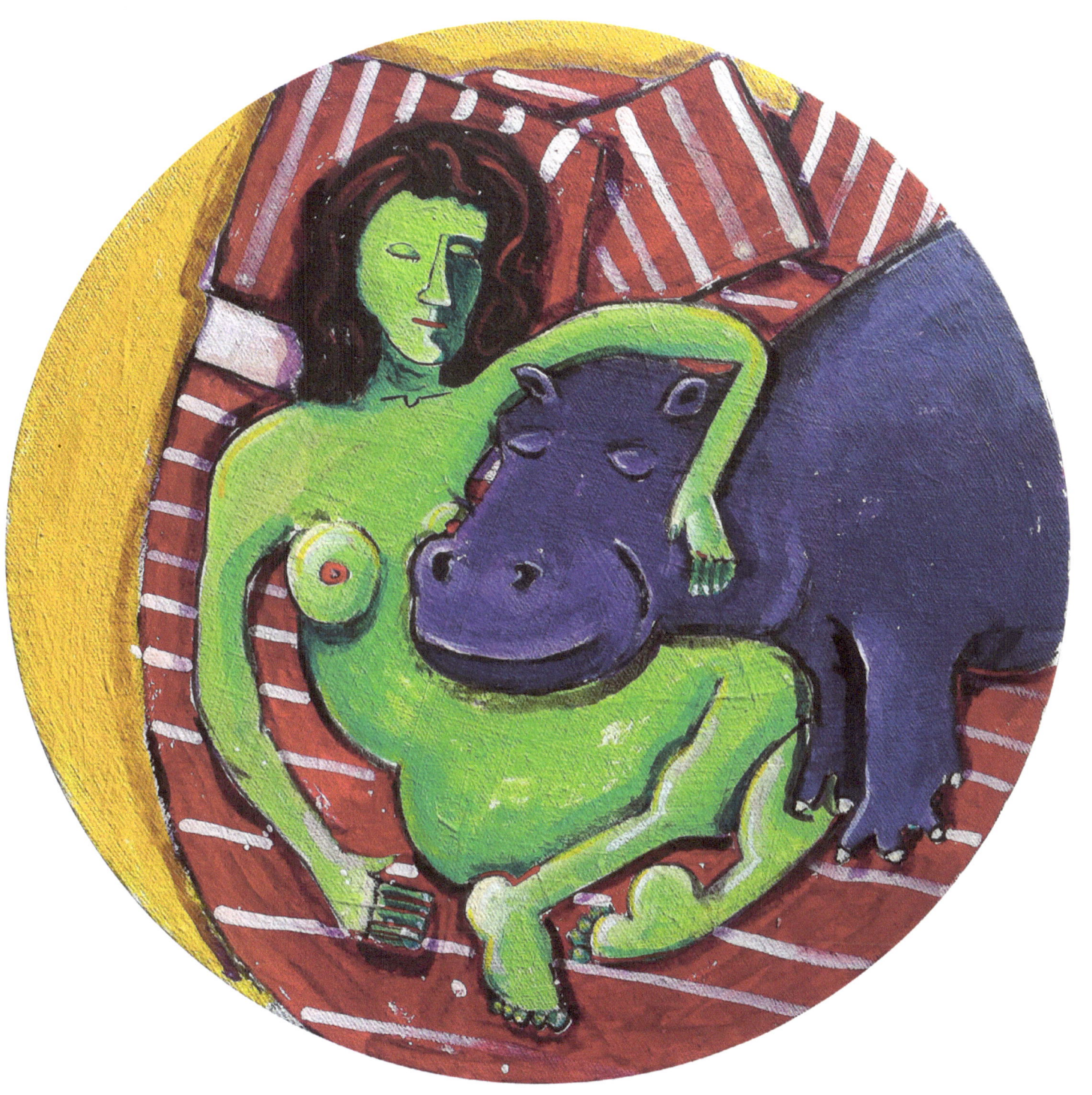

Piglet

Pig in a woman blanket
surrounded by red dotted pearls
make not oink or peep,
as each sleeper curls

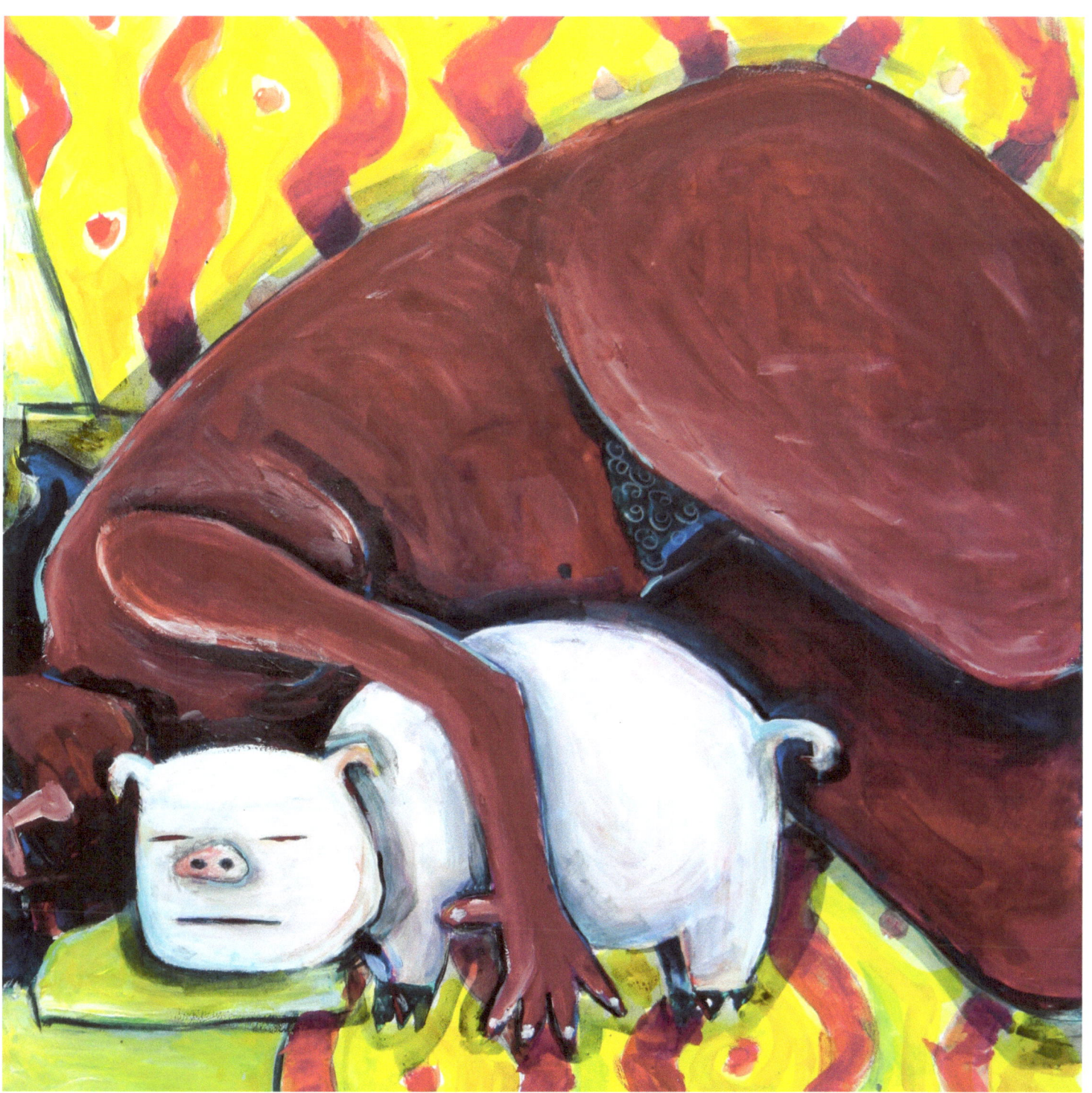

Lemur's Dreamer

A treasure
of an unknowing
Dreamer
for a lemur
Sycophant

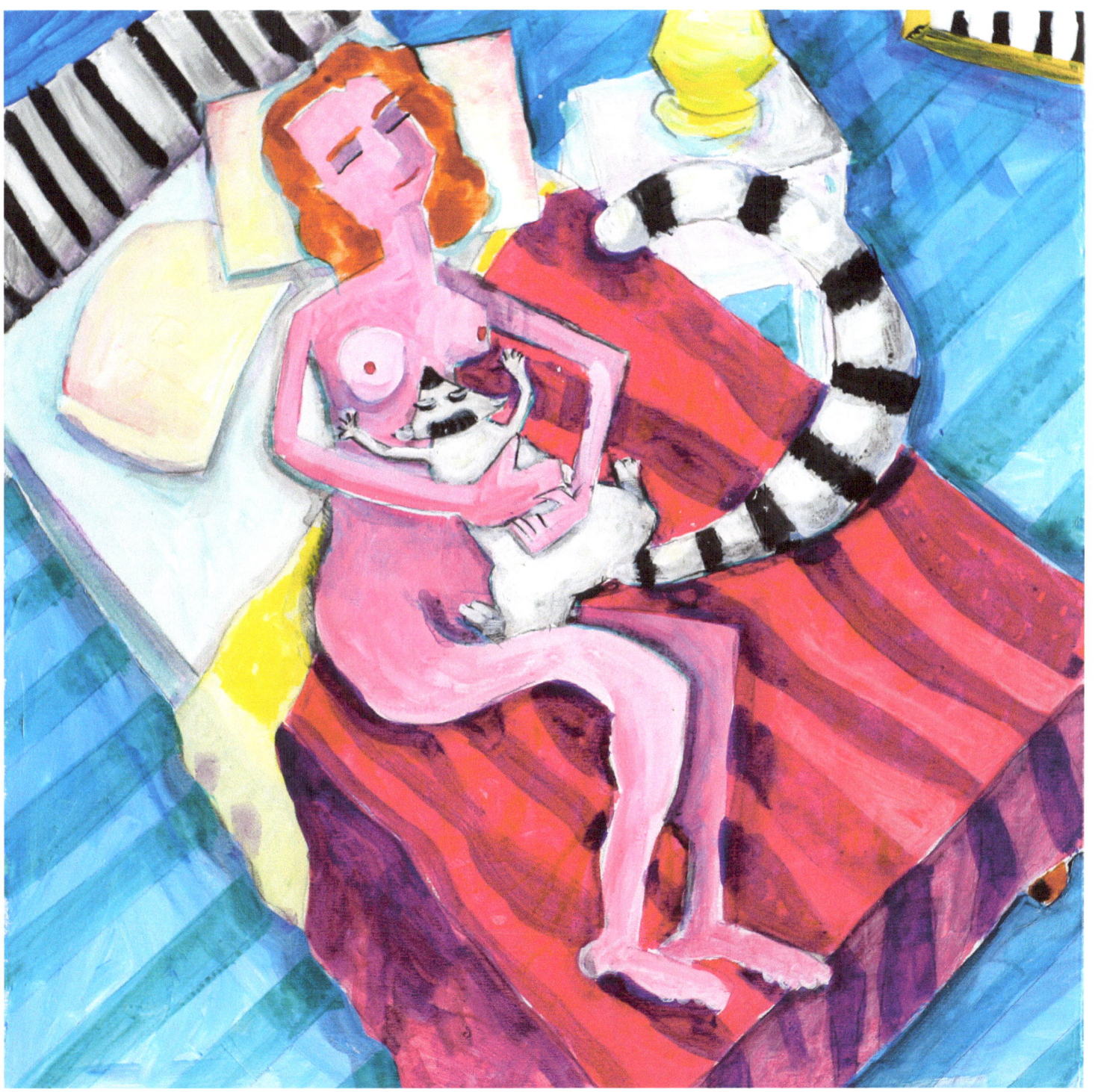

Rocket Rabbit

Light years away
Her Orion arms around bunny
make a bed along the Milky Way

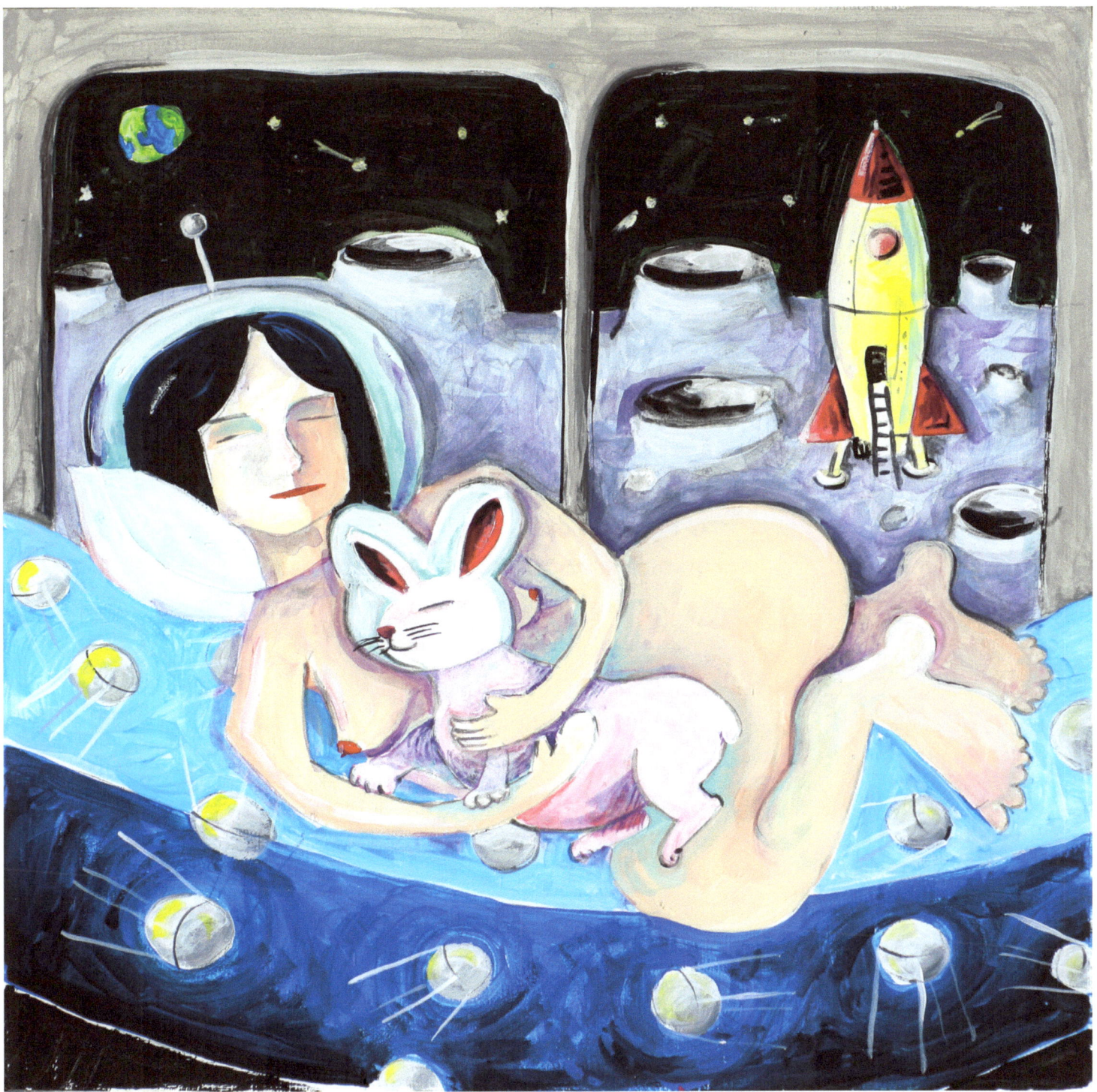

Faceless Platypus

Platypus magnanimous
conked out flat with a cowardly mate
wont make a fuss
when she wakes him up late

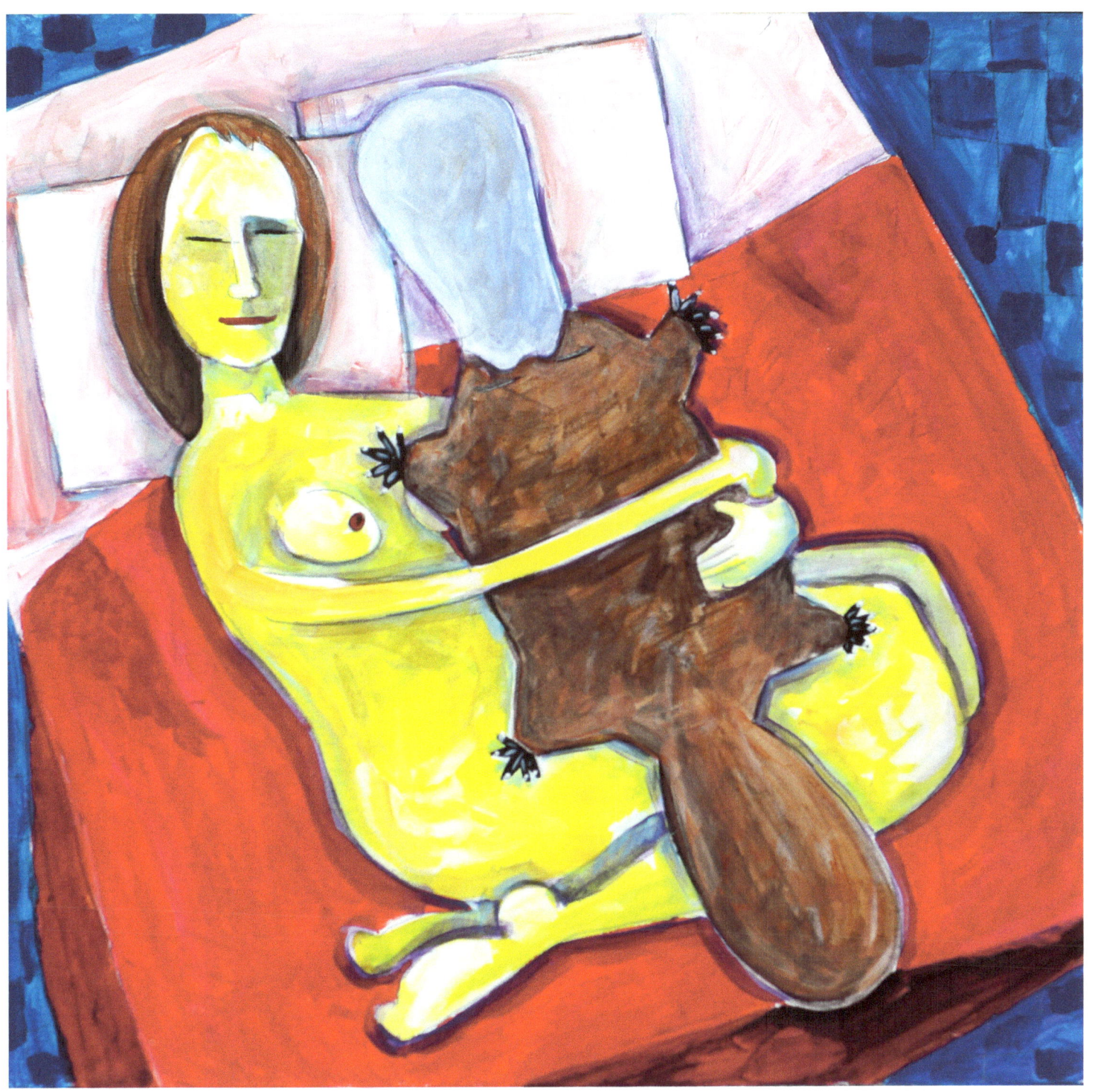

A Celtic Goddess

Catatonic dusk to dawn and dusk again
one may wonder
where sleep begins and where it ends

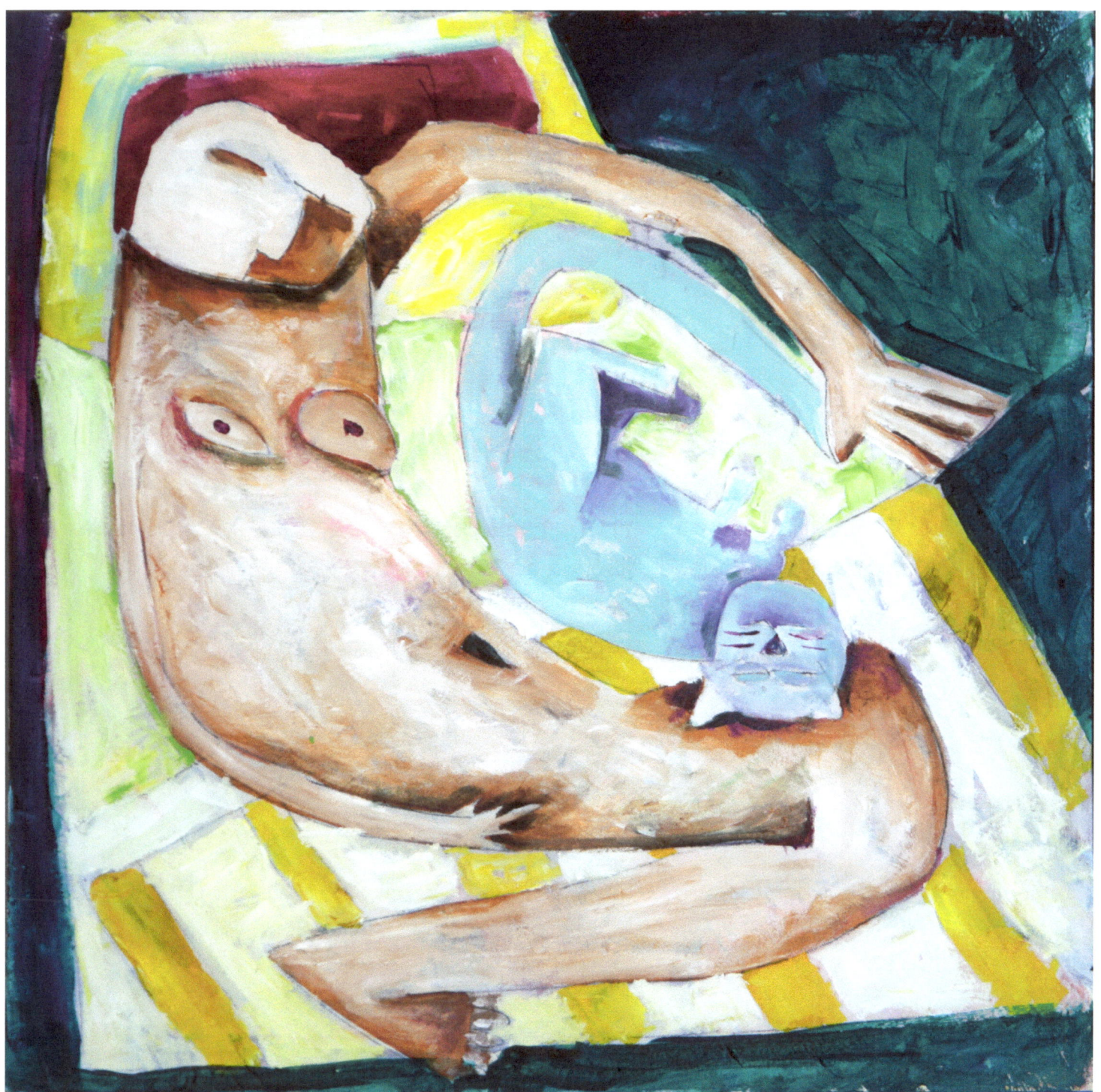

Horse Sense

A horse can trot
dead asleep in dead of night
but makes a bed for two
a little bit tight

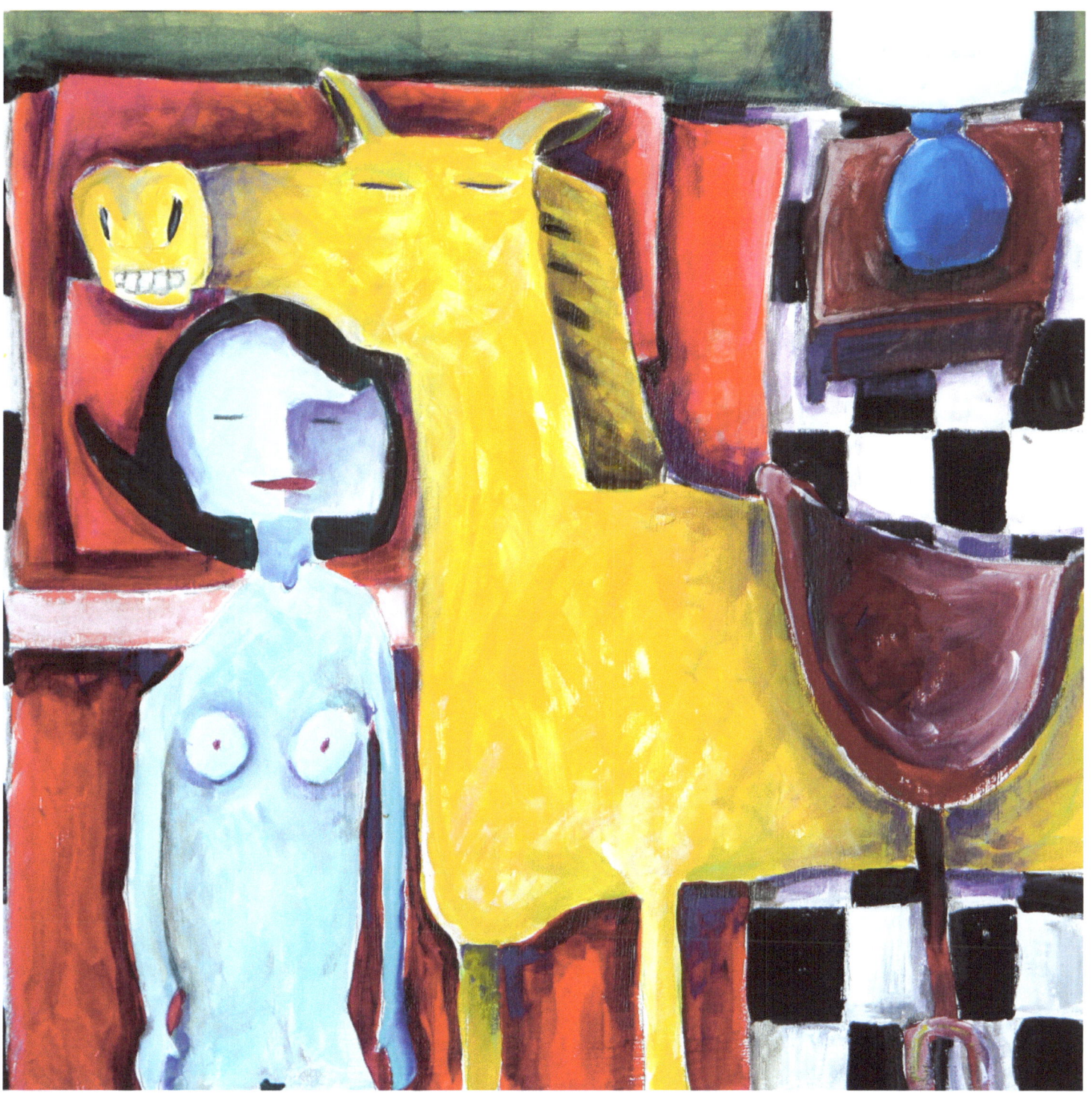

Take Out

Drunk off delivery bamboo
a pink contortionist and a panda
each bit off more than they could chew

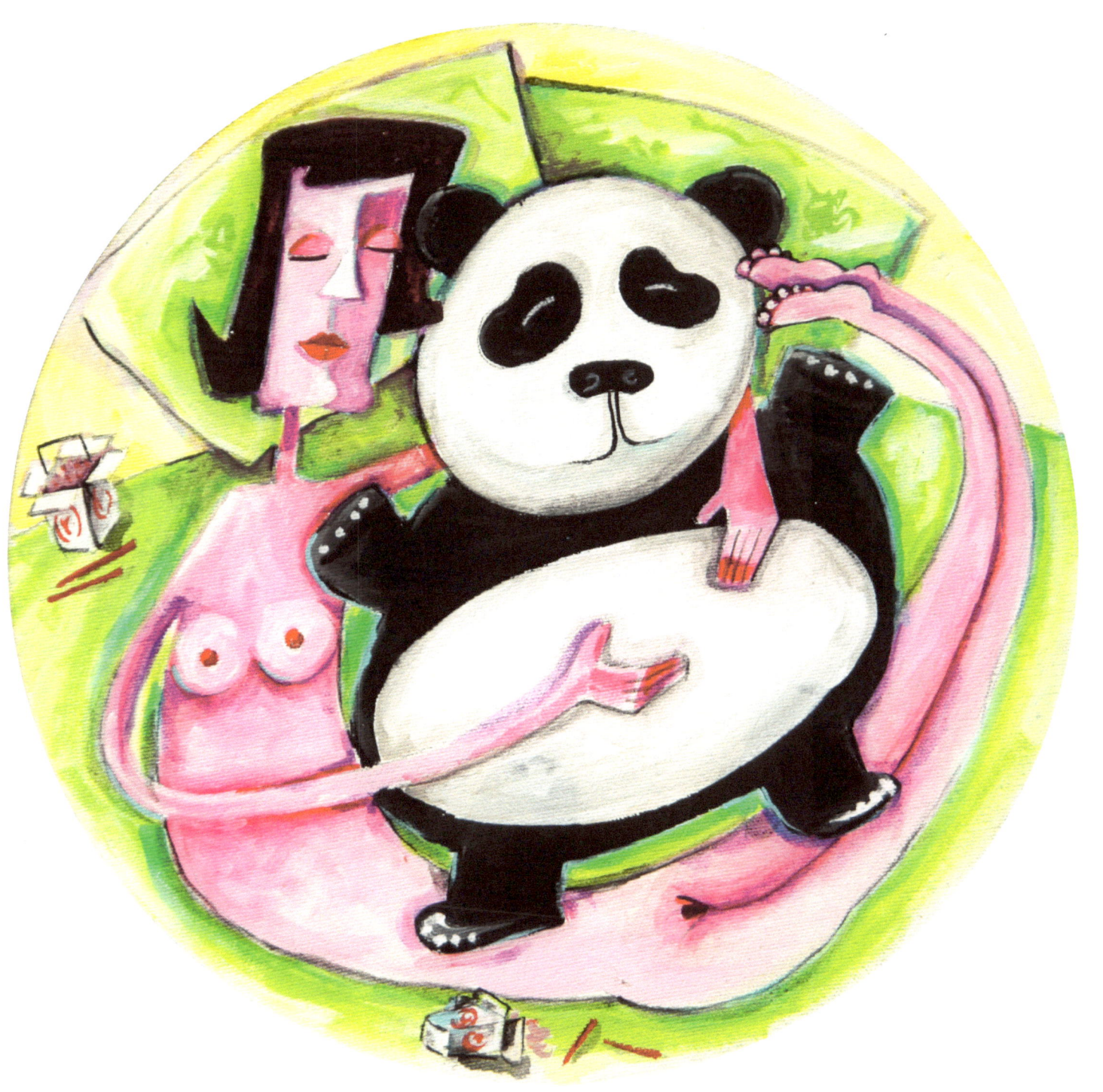

Aquarium ZZZZZZZZZ

A waterbed makes waves for two, but
if a dugong tail won't swim you to sleep,
flippers will do

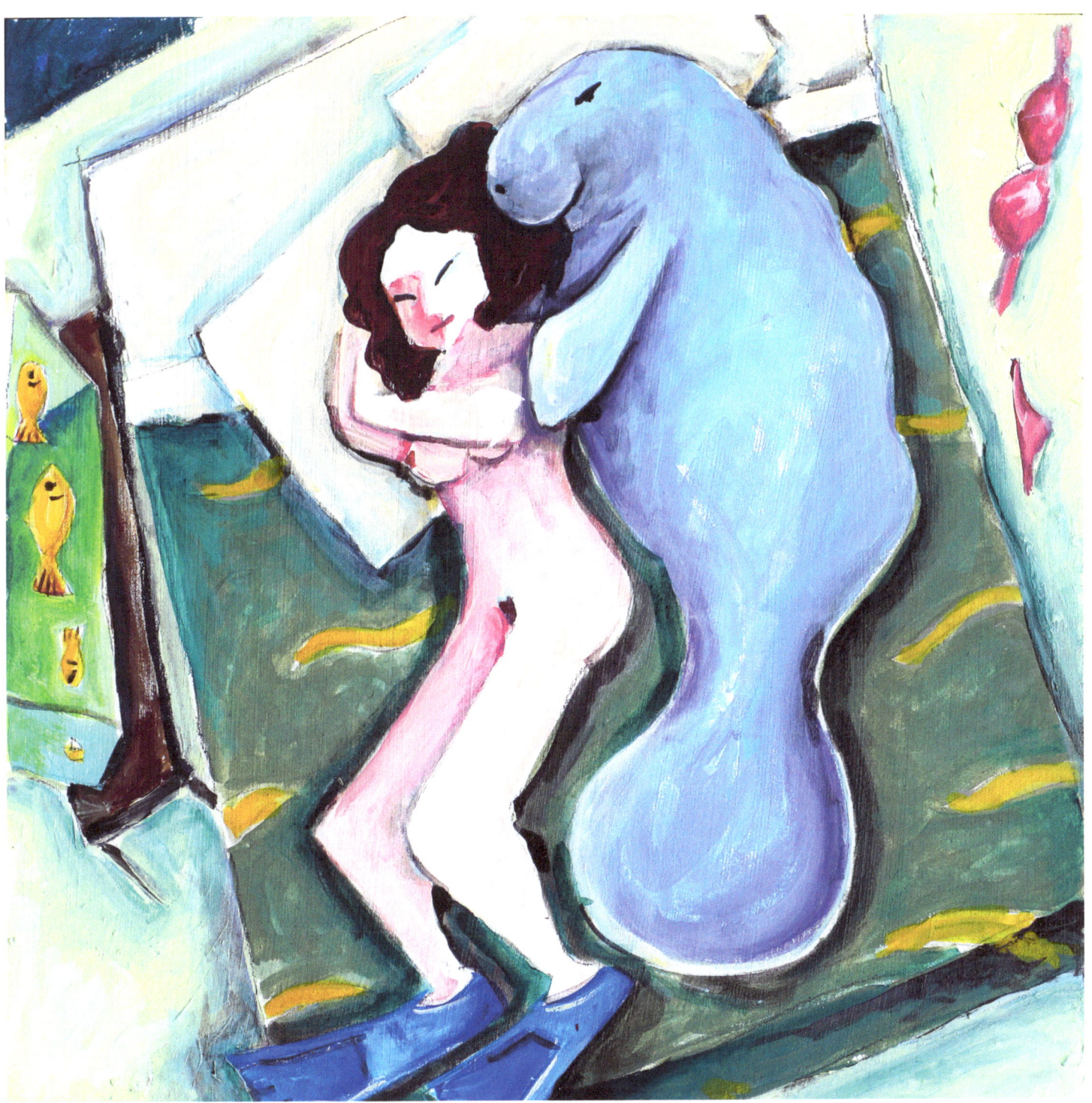

Best Friend

A best friend at long last
who never snores
lets her sleep away the past
and forget her chores

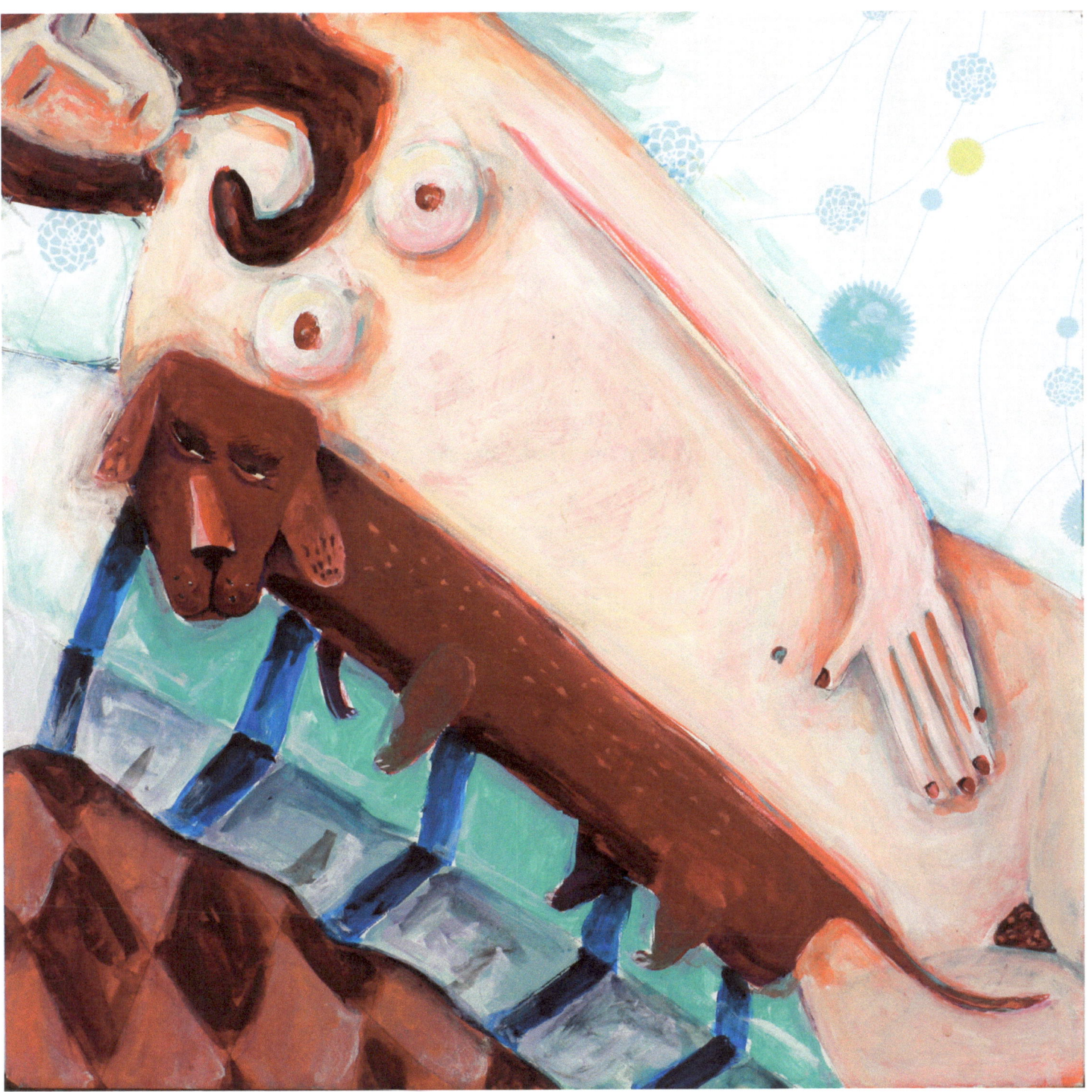

Mermaid Spoon

A Dauphine of France
in a coat of arms her Dolphin
a land-locked embrace

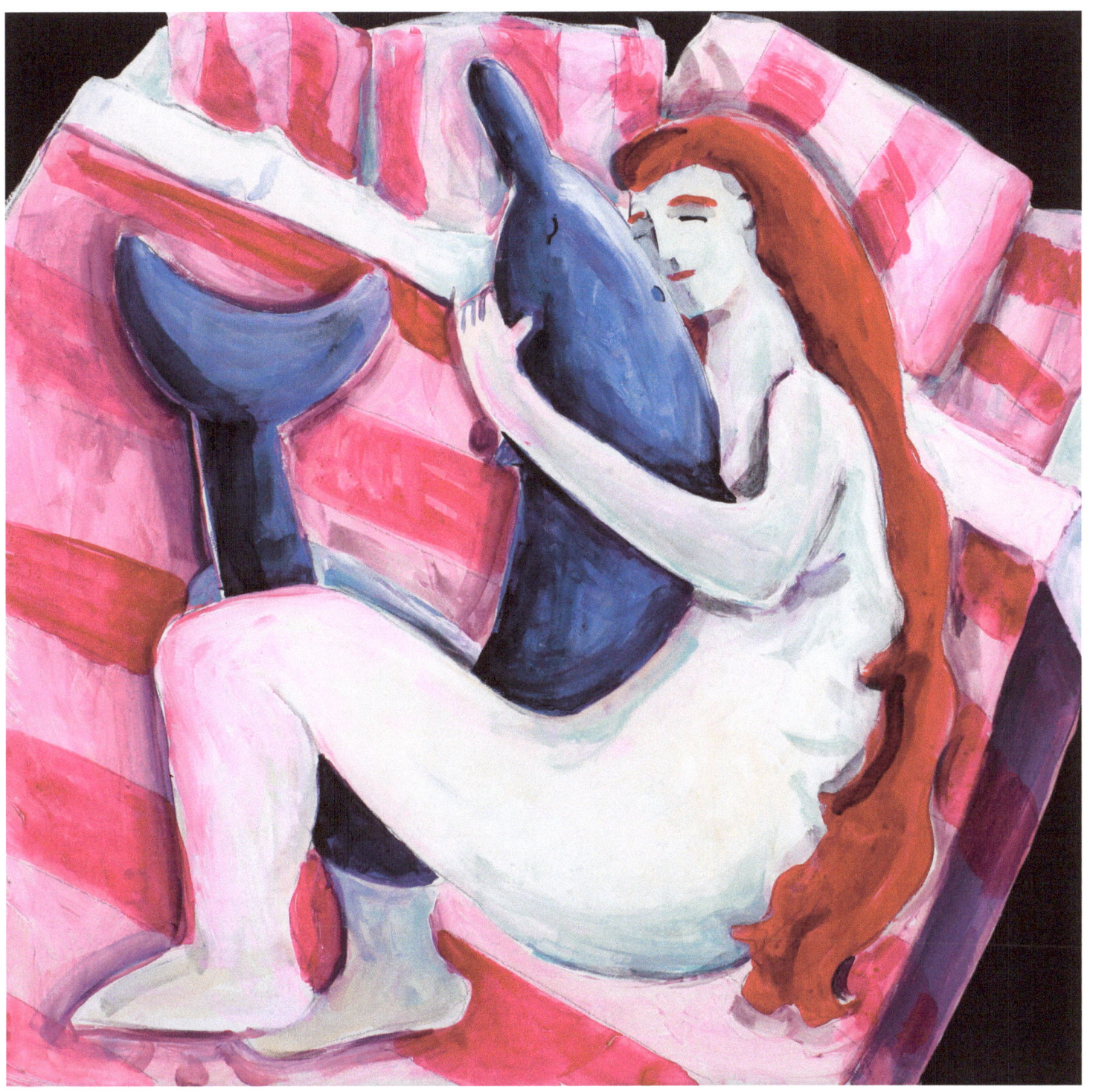

Bad Reputation

On a jailhouse island both marooned,
a notorious thief
and her accomplice raccoon

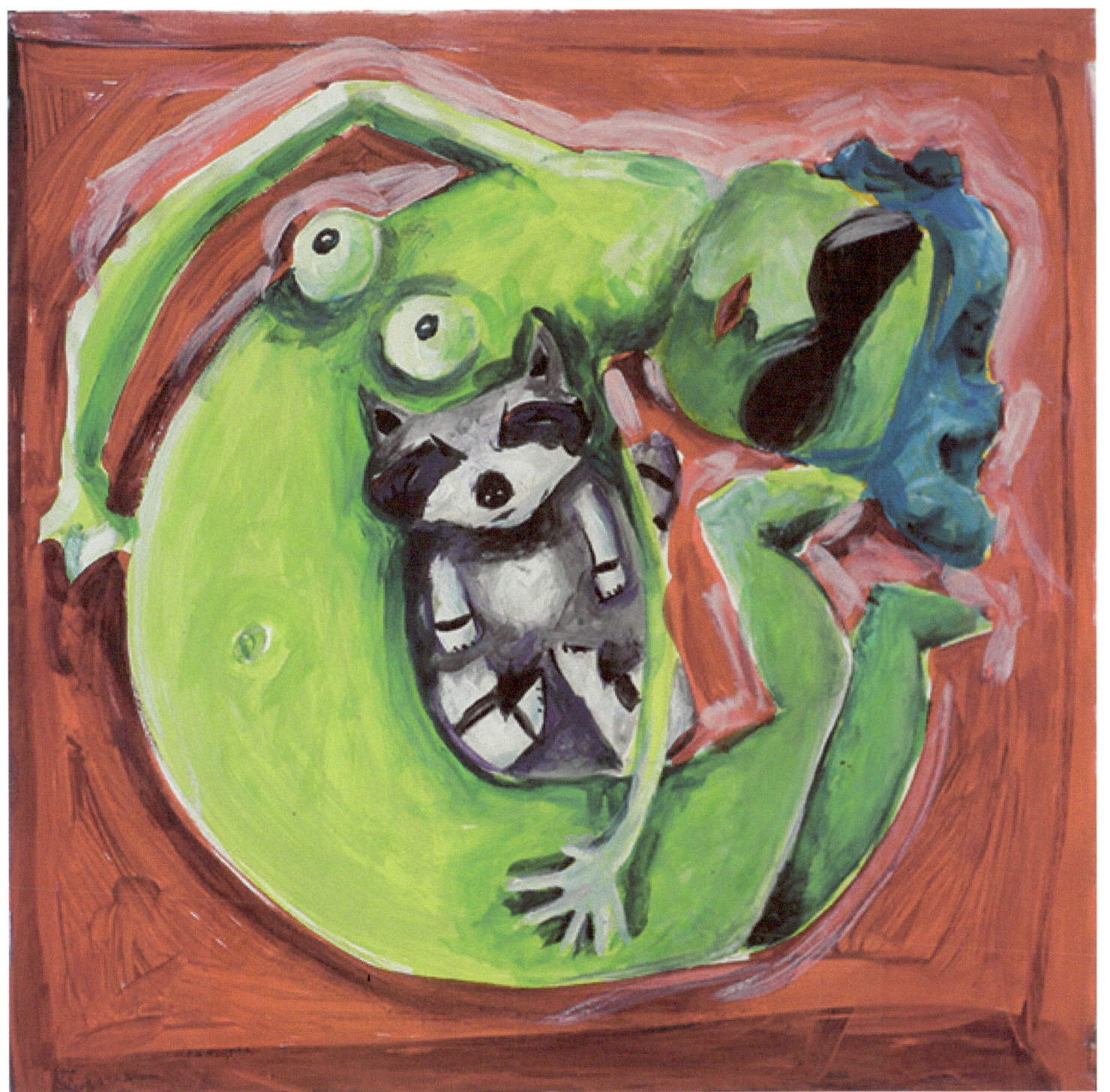

Bedtime Snack

Ferret nibbles on damsel's toes
so from night til dawn
her feet don't show

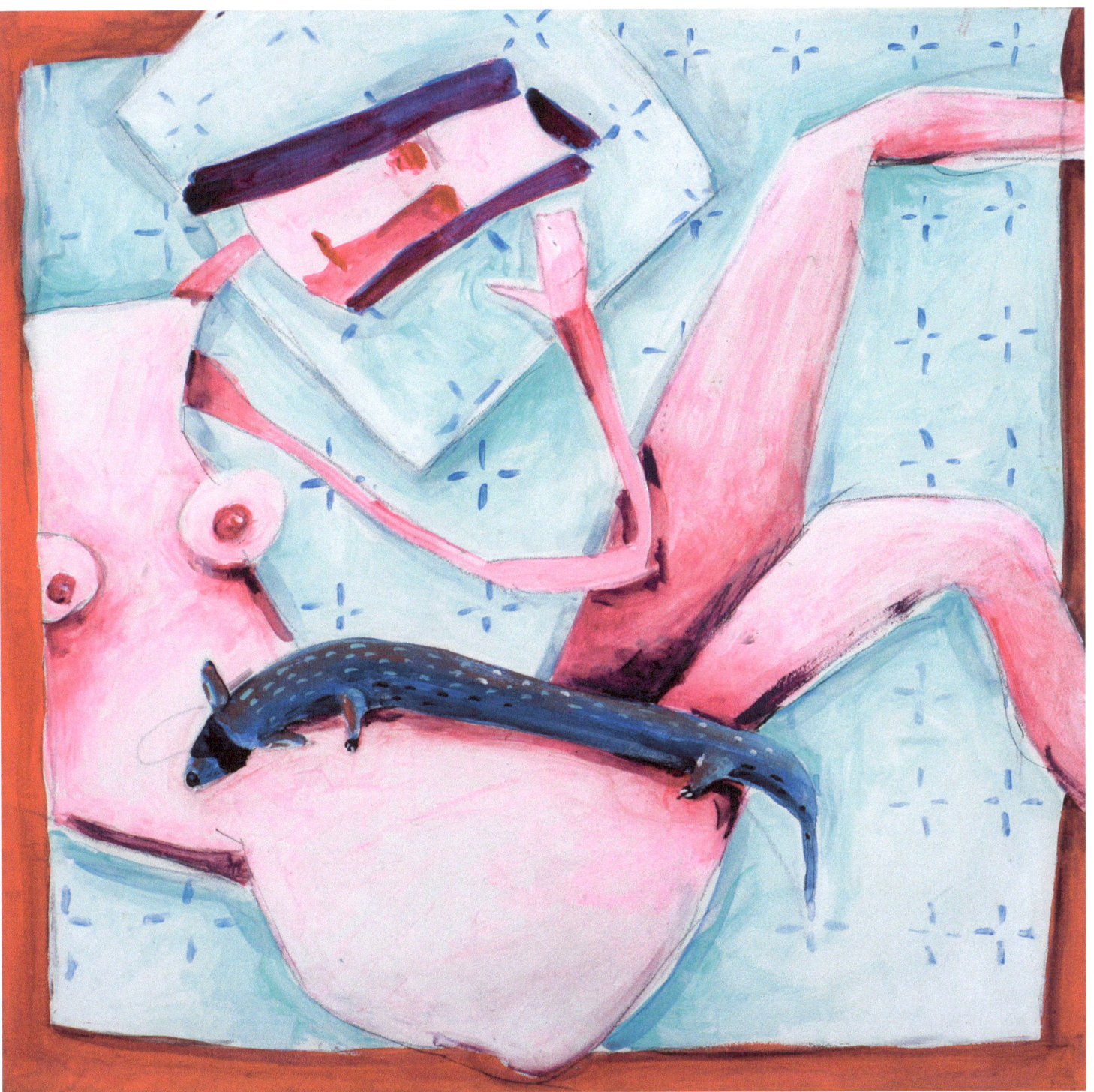

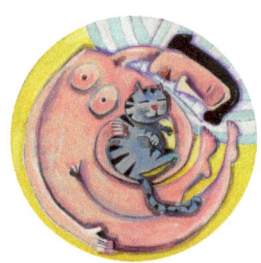

The end